Complicated Child?

Simple Options

Becki Linderman

Disclaimer

The intent of this book is to share the personal stories and opinions of a group of concerned parents. This book is not to be construed as a treatment program or claim of cure for any disease or medical condition. Please do not take it as such. Readers are encouraged to use discretion and to formulate individual opinions. The products that are discussed in this book provide superior nutritional support only. The opinions expressed are just that, personal opinions. They are not the express opinion of Cell Tech. The information herein is not intended to replace the advice of the qualified health practitioner of your choice.

The following phrases are trademarked by Cell Tech: Energy For Life™, Alpha Sun™, Omega Sun™, Spectrabiotic™, Super Blue Green™ Algae, Energy For Fun™, and Energy For Change™.

Cell Tech Approval #115979.

Ransom Hill Press
PO Box 325
Ramona, CA 92065-0325
(800) 423-0620

Complicated Child? Simple Options
Third Edition

Cover Art — Brandee Sonner

Acknowledgment

I dedicate this book first and foremost to my son T.J. It is his life that I share with you, it is his gift of hope that I share for your children. Secondly, to my daughter Brandee, who is my gift of unconditional love. She has loved T.J. through the worst of his problems when at most times she was the brunt of his distress. She has been a constant beacon. I thank my husband, Vern, for being a wonderful step-dad in the face of challenges so great that it would have been easier for him to turn around and walk away — but he didn't. Thanks to my mom, Kathy, and my dad, Lionel, for always being there to pick up the pieces of my broken spirit and for nursing me back to health.

I thank the families who have shared their stories with you in this book. Their lives have touched mine deeply and I know they will touch you. My network of family and friends is large and I thank them all *(you know who you are)*. My deepest appreciation and love goes out to my partner in life, Jeannie. Without her this book would still be just thoughts in my head. Thanks Jeannie for your gentle push.

Ransom Hill Press, Polly, and Summer, your faith in me and this project will forever be appreciated. Thanks for taking a chance! Tony, thanks for your editing support. Nicole, thanks for the technical support. It's been nice working with my brother and my sister on this endeavor.

My final thanks go out to Cell Tech and the little green life form known as Super Blue Green Algae.

Contents

Introduction

The concept for this book came strictly out of need. Many people have heard or read the algae story about my son T.J. I have received phone calls from people across the country who want to talk to me personally or who would like me to share my experiences with someone else who is in need. Believe me, the need is greater than we can even imagine. I love sharing the sense of hope I now have with anyone who is looking for answers. Many people and children are living similar stories. Many people are desperate for even a glimmer of hope and success. My story is one of hope and success for T.J., me, and my family. Just maybe, it can be a glimmer for someone else, some other child.

I would love to talk to you all personally. I feel connected to everyone I have shared with. Unfortunately, it is not possible for me to share my voice with all of you on a personal level. I have a marriage, young family to raise, and business to run that consume most of my time. What I can do is give a part of myself to you in this book.

Let me begin by sharing my personal story with you. You need to know where I come from and why I feel so compelled to share it. I will also be sharing some thoughts about the process of awareness that I have gone through. I have had a tremendous amount of support along the way from family, friends, teachers, and other professionals. I have formed unions with many other families in similar situations. There are other children's stories that have had a direct effect on my life. With their parents' permission, I will also be sharing these children's lives with you.

Since the first edition of this book was published, I have

been repeatedly asked, "How are the children in the book doing now, a year later?"

It is therefore with immense pleasure that in this new, revised edition I am able to share updates on the progress of some of these children.

Unfortunately, I was not able to make timely contact with all of the parents, and a couple of the children no longer eat algae. The family lives of the children no longer eating algae seem to be a struggle. I send them my love and support no matter what their circumstances. These are the families who need it the most.

Finally, I thank all of you who have supported my efforts in sharing this book and the spark of hope that awaits. I've been able to touch many people and hopefully many children's lives.

T.J.

Life with my son T.J. started out with a lot of intensity. Unplanned pregnancy, three months of morning sickness, full time college classes, and a shaky marriage seemed to be predictors of what was to come. The birth was a long process. Twenty-one hours after it began, I had a beautiful baby boy. It was as if his little soul knew how difficult life would be for him, so he delayed it as long as possible. Once here, if you looked past the colic, quick temper, and "no-napping," he was a delight — a very bright, curious, nonstop explorer. I had my hands full. My grandparents moved to the town that I lived in to take care of T.J. so that I could finish college. I graduated when he was eleven months old.

My husband, T.J., and I then moved to my husband's farm. Life went on pretty normally for a while. I learned that you just didn't leave T.J. alone, because before he walked well, he climbed. I remember walking into the kitchen one day when he was about twelve months old only to find him on top of the refrigerator searching the upper cupboard for whatever he could find. He was completely delighted at his accomplishment. Heart-stoppage became a trademark of mine. I have to admit that this still happens today, but on rare occasions. T.J. was also aggressive and at times downright mean. I just wrote it off as, "He's *all* boy, all right! Farm boys are supposed to be tough!" T.J. demanded most of my time and energy.

My marriage was difficult. We were young and my husband displayed many of the same behaviors that I saw in my son. I didn't have the energy to cope with both. I left my husband and moved back to my parents' home with T.J. He had just turned two.

While I was trying to heal a broken heart, I fell sick. After a few days of nausea, my mom asked, "Is it possible that you may be pregnant?" I knew it was just my nerves from having left my husband. My mom has great instinct, though, and insisted that I see a doctor. Guess what? I was pregnant. I had always wanted two children, so I was thrilled. I just knew that God wouldn't give me another child as rambunctious as T.J., especially now that I was facing uncertainty about my marriage.

During my pregnancy I enjoyed T.J. It was just the two of us and we relished the closeness. I would watch him and be amazed at his intelligence and energy. I wasn't even aware of how a second child would challenge this relationship.

When my daughter was born I knew God had answered my prayers. She was beautiful. A healthy baby in all respects. This was another triumph in my life. Unfortunately, I wasn't able to enjoy this as much as I would have liked. My brilliant little boy became an angry big brother.

I couldn't leave T.J. alone with Brandee for fear he might hurt her. He became a master manipulator of mom's affection. When Brandee would start to cry for some unknown reason (probably known to T.J.) he would turn on the charm and brilliance. He knew how to get me sidetracked. I was lucky in that Brandee was, and still is, a completely loving child and so easy to deal with. She loved her brother no matter how treacherous he was.

When T.J. started preschool, the adventure began. Most parents at the school plays and programs watched their children dance, sing, and perform in skits. I watched T.J. stare at the lights, rub his nose, toss his head around, and dance when everyone else was still. To my dismay, I listened as strange bodily sounds seemed to erupt from his mouth. When parents would whisper, "Who is that child?" I sat in stone silence. Then at the end he would come running up to me with this tremendous sparkle in his eyes. How could I not love this child who was so full of it? Even though at times I didn't know what *it* was.

My husband and I had been trying to work on our marriage again since the birth of our daughter. The stress of a failing marriage finally came to a close. I divorced the kids' dad when they were five and three. This was a difficult transition for T.J. He took on the blame for the marriage not working out. He really believed that if he had been a better kid, the divorce wouldn't have happened. I loved and supported T.J. as much as I could. We were all blessed when another man came into our lives who began to fill the void. I remarried months later.

School became harder and harder for T.J. Reports from his teachers were always the same: *"T.J. is so smart but he just can't do the work. He gets frustrated and throws temper tantrums."* Yet we all knew that T.J. could be a charmer. He had gotten this far on his intelligence and wit. The thing that broke my heart was that as time went on T.J. became sadder and sadder. He was extremely hard on himself because he knew how smart he was and yet he couldn't do the work. I remember driving home with the kids one day after school and T.J. looked at me with tears in his eyes, ready to give up, because school was so hard. Life in general was getting hard for T.J. to cope with.

When T.J. was in first grade, his frustration level was so high that he began banging his head on the desk while the teacher and other children looked on in fear. His IQ was tested and he scored a high 136, yet he was failing in school. It got to the point where we knew we had to intervene. We were told our options for finding something to help T.J. function were limited to medication. Even with the addition of prescription drugs (which I considered extreme intervention), T.J.'s self esteem continued to deteriorate. A couple of days before Mother's Day in 1990 I received a call at work from his first grade teacher. Again my heart stopped in fearful anticipation of what was going on now. In tears she said, "Becki, you need to come in after school today. T.J. is okay, but you need to see something."

Luckily I didn't have too long to wait before I left to see her. I walked into the classroom and his teacher looked so sad. We sat down and she showed me the Mother's Day card T.J. had made for me. Tears welled in my eyes as I looked at a drawing of our house, T.J. standing beside it with a bloody knife in his hands and blood dripping from his heart. He had written underneath, *"For Mother's Day my gift to you is that I die so your life could be better."* I was so confused because I loved this child beyond belief. Was I not doing enough?

That began our roller coaster ride down a road of counseling, behavior modification programs, school meetings, tests, seminars, and everything else that goes hand in hand when working with a child with severe emotional problems and hyperactivity. In the ensuing years, various actions would work for a while, not work, or cause severe side effects.

One of the behaviors we saw in T.J. was extreme anxiety. Fire prevention week at school was a nightmare for T.J. He didn't sleep for two weeks straight, staying up at night so he could be sure to hear the fire alarm. All the coaching we did to reassure him was to no avail. He was determined to get our family out alive. Our two-story house had fire alarms upstairs and down. The kids' rooms were upstairs. At four o'clock in the morning one night he came running and screaming downstairs that the fire alarm was going off. My husband and I woke up to T.J.'s screams. When we calmed him down we could hear the faint chirp of a low-battery warning in the downstairs alarm. T.J. was exhausted! We all were exhausted!

Another behavior we saw was obsessive patterns. He ended up getting chicken pox. He wasn't extremely sick, but he almost went crazy with the itching of the pox. He couldn't leave them alone. Needless to say, months later he still had scabs on his arms and hands that always became a focal point of his attention. We had done everything possible to try to get him to stop. I would wrap his arms and hands to protect them. He would pull the wrapping off, scratching and crying that he couldn't help it. When I saw him picking at the scabs I would just grab him and hug him tight. I would hold his wiggling body until his attention switched to something else. I became hyper-aware of his every move.

Those are just a couple of stories among many. We were using every resource that we thought was available to us. As a result, by the time T.J. was ten years old we had tried just about everything to help him live a normal life. I did everything in my power to help him within the established practices for working with his problems. We didn't see any major success. The emotional turmoil at times was almost more than my family could bear. Only a thread held us together, but I was determined not to lose my son or my family.

T.J.'s behavior continued to get worse, more negative, and school became an unending list of failures for him. His IQ kept pulling him through so that he passed each grade level. Almost everyone he came in contact with had a difficult time dealing with him. Underneath all of this little boy's negativity and pain, I saw a child who was trying so hard just to function from day to day that it broke my heart.

In April of 1993, T.J. began to develop severe motor dysfunction. We sought help for him, and soon his motor dysfunction dissipated, though his emotional problems continued. We were advised that he should see specialists in Salt Lake City who might help his anxiety and depression.

Eventually, his emotional problems reached critical mass

in October of 1993. The specialists in Salt Lake told us that T.J. needed to be institutionalized, at least for a while. He was only ten. The hardest thing I have ever done in my life was to kiss him good-bye and walk out, leaving him behind three locked doors. I wouldn't be able to see him for over two weeks. Extensive testing was done, but no biological dysfunction revealed itself in his brain. His emotional problems persisted. The specialists made more changes, such as implementing a very rigid behavior modification program, and yet they still offered me little hope of success. Finally, the experts suggested that T.J. needed extensive time in an institution, which of course was not financially feasible. They also felt that if T.J. didn't improve, he was headed toward eventual placement in a juvenile facility.

After a month, T.J. came home. He was fine for about two weeks, though still struggling with his emotional problems. Again, his behavior deteriorated and our home life was a struggle. I was exhausted and just wanted my son back. I knew in the deepest part of my soul that he was a wonderful child, but I no longer saw any sparkle in his eyes. What I saw was blank and lifeless. I gathered up what strength I had left and decided to make a change. I let go of some of the methods we had tried over the past four years, but I had no idea where to go next.

This is where Cell Tech comes in. A very dear friend of mine knew someone who was a Cell Tech distributor. This friend was so impressed with the algae that she set up an appointment for me to be introduced to Super Blue Green Algae (SBGA). I was interested specifically for T.J. I thought, why not? He has been through so much, how could something natural hurt? I signed up as a new distributor. The cost was minimal compared to the huge amount of money we had already spent over the years.

The night I received the first algae shipment, T.J. wanted

to try the Liquid Omega Sun, so I let him. I saw a child who couldn't get himself to function well enough to do household chores or homework suddenly get up and single-handedly fix our entire dinner, set the table, eat, and then clean up the dishes afterward! I watched in complete amazement and asked him, "What's going on?"

He said, "I have all this energy, I might as well do something constructive with it." I picked my chin up off of the floor and continued to watch him. After cleaning up, he put a rock-and-roll tape in his boom-box, turned up the volume, and proceeded to sing his math problem solutions as he wrote them down! I can't begin to tell you how stunned I was at what I was watching. I had hope where I once felt hopeless. Most importantly, I watched my son have some success. His initial program consisted of enzymes, then Omega Sun, then Alpha Sun. We went slowly and monitored him closely.

For several months after he began eating the algae, we really didn't know from one day to the next what to expect. Some days he would function very well, but some days were extremely hard. I had become so used to juggling things that it was natural for me to work with the amount of algae I gave T.J. in trying to obtain optimum levels. His body cleansed for months. The miracle was that his eyes began to sparkle again. I was ecstatic.

T.J. was able to finish fifth grade, but it had been a struggle. The school had a full-time teacher's aide available, and they tried to do the best they could within their established system to work with us. T.J. also began to see a psychologist who was able to make a small connection with him. This was a huge breakthrough because by this time T.J. trusted no one. This man was not "conventional" and supported my evolving belief that T.J. was not the disturbed child we had been led to believe, but was a child with many gifts. T.J. was not a lost cause who needed to be institutionalized. His mind and body had just been so unhealthy that as he started to improve with the algae and counseling, everyone we knew saw the profound change in him.

The summer of 1994 was a wonderful time for us. T.J. had become calmer and that had an easing effect on the whole family. He began to communicate with us in a whole new way. He shared with us verbally not only his pains but his joys. I guess you could call it an awakening. I began to search out other alternative health methods. We connected with some wonderful people focused on nutrition and what Cell Tech is all about. They have really supported us in our efforts.

As T.J. became healthier, I began to witness events that may startle most people, but I knew them to be true for T.J. Not only did he become more perceptive of life (coming out of the fog he had known for years), but he began to perceive life energies around him too. It was not uncommon for him to see and describe energy fields around people and things. I don't want to offend any particular belief system, I only tell you this because the fact is that my child's life went from constant negative events and feelings to a life of health and wonderment. That summer the chaos we had all become accustomed to was gone!

T.J. started sixth grade and was able to function fairly well in the regular system! He was fortunate to have a teacher who valued him for who he was and who did not consider his past a factor. This teacher helped T.J. begin to believe in himself again. With a lot of strong guidance, love, and algae, T.J. became a pretty normal preadolescent boy. The teachers and counselors concur that sixth grade was his most successful year. They even admitted to me that his eating algae was a key factor.

In February of 1995, I received a call from T.J.'s third grade teacher. She had seen T.J. out on his bike a couple of

Would you like to receive our catalog? Ransom Hill Press carries:

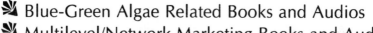 Blue-Green Algae Related Books and Audios
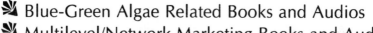 Multilevel/Network Marketing Books and Audios
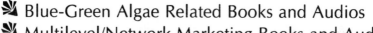 An exclusive collection of beautifully designed
   business-building postcards, t-shirts, and gift items

Ransom Hill Press
1-800-423-0620

Please call our 800 number to request a free catalog.
Or, tear out and mail the reply card below.

Please mail me your catalog.

I will also receive FREE the "Dear Venus" column for one year.
An exclusive from Ransom Hill Press.

Name: _____

Address: _____

City: _____ State: _____ Zip: _____

What MLM company are you with? _____

Comments: _____

Please mail my friend a catalog too.

Name: _____

Address: _____

City: _____ State: _____ Zip: _____

What MLM company are you with? _____

Comments: _____

BUSINESS REPLY MAIL
FIRST-CLASS MAIL   PERMIT NO. 361   RAMONA CA

POSTAGE WILL BE PAID BY ADDRESSEE

RANSOM HILL PRESS
PO BOX 325
RAMONA CA 92065-9932

weeks earlier and had had a very pleasant conversation with him. He told her he was eating Super Blue Green Algae. She wanted me to know how great she thought he looked and acted. She said she could tell immediately that his body was clean and healthy because his eyes were so clear and bright.

In March of 1995 we moved to Montana. It was a new start for all of us, but especially for T.J. His new school welcomed him with expectations of success. It was the first time in four years that he was expected to perform regular work in a regular classroom without extensive intervention. At the annual school spring concert, I admit that I sat on the edge of my chair in anticipation of what I might witness T.J. doing this time. As luck would have it, he stood in the first row at the front of the stage in full view of everyone. I held my breath as I watched him stare into the bright stage lights and then stare blankly into the audience. I was ready for anything, but then he remembered to sing a few verses. He didn't fall off the stage. He made it through the whole performance with only a few strange eye-blinking episodes. I sat back and breathed a sigh of relief and giggled as I realized how far we had come.

He is now in a regular seventh grade class. We as a family have come to appreciate T.J. for who he is. He is still a nonstop explorer. He is completely unique and dances to his own tune. T.J. is a gifted writer and extremely artistic. The charm he used so easily when he was very young is back in full swing. Brandee and T.J. now get along better than most siblings. Not only is T.J. healthier, but Brandee is too. She eats the algae as well. She tells me that the things T.J. does to "bug" her just don't seem to get her as mad now. She is coping with life from a much healthier state of mind and believe me, she needed it. If T.J. has challenged anyone's life it has been that of his little sister. We all eat algae. We all need it. Our whole family has grown so much through the hardship that it is our turn to take a deep breath, relax, and share what we have learned with others.

The algae is such an integral part of our lives now. I can't begin to explain how our lives have changed physically as well as spiritually. We feel completely connected to Cell Tech's goals and vision. I have deep gratitude for my Cell Tech family. It can only be expressed as love. Without the algae and the courage it took to make a change, I would not have my family as I now know it. I would not be looking into T.J.'s eyes and seeing the amazing sparkle of life that I now see. Thank you Daryl, Marta, and Cell Tech! I have my son back!

Love,
Becki Linderman

One Year Later

T.J. is certainly one of my greatest teachers. This last year has been a continual unfolding of awareness, not only for T.J. but for myself as well. What a gift we are all given in the children of the world. It is with a light heart and much pride that I tell you that my children are truly amazing! I'm not sure I could have said that as easily three years ago.

At the end of T.J.'s seventh grade year he was elected Student Representative to the Junior High governing body. He stood up in front of the entire student body and gave an impromptu speech about why they should elect him. The response from the student body was amazement at how good his ideas were. They saw his leadership potential. I am glad the students were able to see this side of T.J. because his reputation is still that of "class clown." He is always busting up the class with his quick wit. Of course, this continues to be a challenge for some of his teachers. Not all of them appreciate his humorous discourse. Yet even this challenge is lesser than those of previous years.

For two weeks during summer break, T.J. visited a friend from our old home town. He was pressured by this friend to drink and party. This was the same friend whom T.J. had partied with two and a half years earlier. Yes, at ten years old the kids were experimenting. Why would my son be leery of a little pot and alcohol? For years he had been given some of the most potent medications on the market. What message were we sending to him? Don't do drugs but take these pills so you can behave?

This time T.J. refused to bow down to the pressure and told his friend that he was not interested. This created a rift between the two of them. T.J. was made fun of and ridiculed but he stood his ground. It is my belief that he values his body and mental state more now because of what he has learned over almost three years of eating algae and becoming healthy. He won't let anyone take his algae away!

My daughter Brandee is also learning to value her body. She is blossoming into a beautiful young girl who is full of confidence and pride in her health and her body (attributes that have taken me years to attain). Her personality is as quick-witted as her brothers and she keeps all of us laughing. What a blessing she continues to be as her love just seems to radiate from every pore of her body. Do I believe algae continues to support her being the best she can be? You bet I do!

At one point during the summer, T.J. become bored. Living in a small town can have its drawbacks for a very active kid. He was getting tired of creating trouble by skateboarding in places where he wasn't supposed to be. One day, he came to me and announced that he was going to build a skateboard/rollerblade park and wanted to talk to the town about it. Tongue-in-cheek, I replied that he would probably have to talk to someone at City Hall. I went about my business as T.J. disappeared out the door. I thought he was going skateboarding. In about twenty minutes he burst through the door and said excitedly, "Mom, I'm on the agenda for Tuesday night!"

I laughed! Nothing surprises me these days. I replied, "I guess you better get your presentation ready if you are going before the City Council."

T.J. worked that weekend designing a state-of-the-art skateboard/rollerblade park. It was to be about one thousand square feet. I drafted his design and he asked his dad to help him estimate costs. By Tuesday evening, T.J. was prepared. He knew exactly what he wanted to say. We waited patiently for an hour and a half. The fact that T.J. sat there calm and quiet for that long was in and of itself amazing. Then T.J. stood before the City Council and presented his plan like a pro. I was more nervous than he was. T.J. told the council he would have a donation drive and the park would be nonprofit. He said, "It will help keep kids off the streets and give them something fun to do!"

The council was impressed. Of course, their concern was liability. His hopes were dashed slightly as he was confronted with the reality of government. I am happy to report that he still wants to pursue his vision of a park. The local paper decided to run an article about a twelve year old boy appearing before the City Council. When the reporter came to the house to interview T.J., I told her, "You have no idea but there is a huge story behind the one you are reporting on. Here, read this book." I handed her a copy of this book, *Complicated Child? Simple Options*. The article she then wrote about T.J. was truly wonderful. T.J. told her, "If you want something, you have to go out and try to make it happen." Where do you suppose he learned that? I don't think it came from the people who told him he would not function in society.

T.J. is now in eighth grade. He is going to school in the

system as a regular student. He is on the same disciplinary and academic plan as all the other kids. He is passing all of his classes and continues to improve. I foresee in the near future that the Individual Education Plan he has had since first grade will no longer be needed. Imagine that!

I recently attended a Women's Expo in Salt Lake City where I was scheduled to speak on the topic, "ADD: The Myth." We all know this stands for Algae Deficient Diet, right?

I hadn't been in Salt Lake since I had picked up T.J. from the institution there years ago, so it was uncanny that I would be speaking there three years to the day after I checked him into that hospital. Here was my opportunity to experience tremendous emotional healing of the guilt and pain I had felt. Can you imagine what it was like for me to get up in front of an audience and say, "Three years ago today I wasn't sure if my son would survive. It was the darkest day of my life as I left my ten year old in the psychiatric wing of the institution here in Salt Lake. Now, I am here to share with you my amazing story of hope and success. My son is very much alive and vibrant due in large part to my courage to take a stand and my discovery of a wild-grown, nutritious whole food known as Super Blue Green Algae."

I have no doubt that my children will continue to thrive and grow to be the best that they can be. I am committed to nourishing their bodies with one of the best foods on the planet, Super Blue Green Algae, and nourishing their souls with unconditional love and acceptance. Need I say more!

Love,
Becki Linderman

Options

There is an evolving belief that is now coming into the consciousness of more and more people. It is the belief that we have more control over our own health and well-being than we previously thought. This holds true for us adults, but we need to remember that this is also true for our children. Their lives are completely in our hands. They rely on us to love them, take care of them, and guide them safely into adulthood. This is a hard job! How many of us truly understood what that job would entail? Then, add to that job description a child who is physically, intellectually, emotionally, or socially challenged, and it can seem like an overwhelming proposition.

What I am sharing with you in this book are thoughts about my life as a parent of one of these children. I have had challenges come up that at times seemed insurmountable. The odds were stacked against us in raising T.J. to a healthy adulthood, both in the physical and emotional sense. I am extremely happy to share with you that we are overcoming the odds.

One of the most important characteristics I have gained from all of the experiences with my son is unfailing persistence. Persistence to find something, anything that will help him function in life. I never stop seeking and gaining knowledge. I read everything I can (when I find the time). I continue to expand my own awareness about life, realizing that I don't have all the answers. When I have found something that works, I try to educate those around me to what that may be. I become completely involved in collaborating with the people who are working with T.J. At times I am a nuisance, a squeaky wheel. After all, he is my child. I brought him into this life and I believe he is my responsibility. Besides, who else is going to be his best advocate?

There is one regret I live with: There are many moments that I want to go back in time to change. I regret that I didn't have the courage to follow my gut instincts regarding my child sooner. You know, the feeling in the pit of your stomach that tells you, "This doesn't feel right." When someone who I felt had more knowledge than me would tell me to do something with T.J., even if my gut feeling was saying, "This is not right," I followed his or her direction anyway. I didn't think I was an authority when it came to dealing with my son's problems. I'm not suggesting that anyone who worked with my son did not have his best interest at heart. Some were just educated with a philosophy that was not conducive to getting at the source of his problems, but instead dealt simply with his symptoms. Only when we had reached the end of our options in that approach did I stand up and say, "Enough!" My fear was that I was losing my son, that he might not survive. I was not going to let that happen. What I began to realize was that *I* was the expert when it came to my son. I began to follow my gut instinct, and guess what? My instinct has been right-on ever since. It is my belief that this instinct is divinely guided. I have learned to forgive myself for some of the mistakes along the way. I realize that without my experience just as I lived it, I would not be sharing with you the profound sense of hope that I now feel.

I changed my focus. I began to look at nutrition and natural healing. The whole concept made so much sense to me. Besides, I had already tried everything else. I knew that certain foods seemed to trigger certain behaviors. For instance, one weekend T.J. was hanging out with his friends. He spent every dime he had on candy bars and consumed them all in about one minute. I knew something was wrong when I saw him. His attitude was testing my patience to the limit. The next day he did a tailspin into depression. We talked about what he had done the day before. The only thing we found different from normal was that he had eaten a bunch of chocolate. The light bulbs in my head began to go on. I started to really pay attention to food and its effect on T.J. So began my exploration into a new realm of thinking and doing.

Changing my focus was not an easy process. I had teachers, counselors, family members, and others who did not readily support my decision. They felt I was making a mistake and that I was putting T.J. at extreme risk. That gut instinct of mine overpowered every other doubt that was thrown my way. Now, anyone who had a doubt about what I did is thrilled that I had the courage to persist.

I came to understand that most people don't eat or absorb enough nutrients. As a society, we are so caught up in the fast pace of our lives that highly processed foods have become the norm. Even if we do try to eat whole fruits and vegetables, we can't be sure that their nutrient content is high or viable. The soils these foods are grown in can be very nutrient poor, producing food that is only a fraction of its full natural potential. Eating these foods is a little like eating cardboard. We may have their bulk going into our bodies, but the nutrient value can be almost nonexistent. Our children are being raised in an era of nutritionally poor fast food. They don't stand a chance of having healthy bodies unless we as adults do something about it. Have you seen what most kids eat for lunch at school or snack on when you may not be looking? You may or may not be surprised. The point is that we need to educate ourselves. We all stand a better chance of helping our children if we have an understanding about nutrition and why it is so important in this day and age.

How important is nutrition to brain functioning? There is mounting evidence to support the clear connection between what we take into our bodies and how that in turn affects the delicate chemical balance therein. Is it possible that the subtle balance of chemicals in the brain can be modified by a single meal? There is a close relationship between available nutrients and normal functioning of the brain. Why has there been such an increase in childhood mental illness and behavior problems in recent years? What is happening in our world today? Our environment has changed drastically over the past fifty years. The food we eat, the air we breath, the water we drink is not the same as it once was. We live in a world of chemical saturation now. There is no place on the planet that has not been touched. Consider the fact that the body and brain are made up of molecules derived from food, air, and water. Those are three basic elements that we cannot survive without. It seems likely that our bodies are affected by the changes in our outside environment. It also seems likely that our mental health is affected by these same changes.

The fact that the founder of Cell Tech, Daryl Kollman, began his study into algae because of his compassion for children really hit home with me. As a school teacher, Daryl knew that the children he taught were steadily losing their learning skills. His belief was that this trend was connected to the decreasing quality of their diets. Initially, Daryl thought the algae was a good source of nutrition to help children's diets, but he came to believe that algae is the most important natural source of nutrients on the planet today. He is a man whose vision I share. The more I learned about the algae, the more I realized that perhaps the answer I was looking for was very simple. We have all been given a tremendously simple gift. Super Blue Green Algae is a wild-grown organic food. Nature is the farmer. All the necessary ingredients for vibrant growth exist without man's assistance. The algae lives up to its full potential. I am a firm believer in the innate intelligence of nature. The body recognizes that the algae is a natural food, and in the body's infinite wisdom, it uses what nutrients, minerals, amino acids, and proteins it needs, where it needs them, and when.

It is not my intention to give you all the facts about nutrition. There are many wonderful resources available to you if you have the desire to explore this issue in depth. Some of these are listed in the back of this book. Remember, I am just a parent sharing my experience. If I could give you all a gift, it would be expanded awareness of your challenging child. That awareness includes many facets, one of which is the need for developing an understanding of your child's bodily and nutritional needs. This is the awareness that led me to add Super Blue Green Algae to T.J.'s diet.

All of this new awareness and knowledge would have been for naught if I hadn't seen a change in T.J. with the addition of algae to his life. I saw glimpses of a healthy child right away. I won't kid you. At first I saw only fleeting moments of health and well being. Even fleeting, these moments offered me more hope to grasp onto than I had felt in five years. I persisted! I watched his behavior evolve from a very negative state to a more positive one. I saw calmness come over him. I saw the sparkle return to his eyes. At this point, no one could have convinced me that the addition of algae to T.J.'s diet was not giving his body something it needed.

I don't want you to think that adding algae to our diets is all we have done. Algae is not a cure all or quick fix. It just happens to be one facet among many relating to our health and well being. T.J. has been a wonderful gift to me in expanding the possibilities of acceptance. T.J. is unique. All of us are. Right now in our society there are so many children screaming for acceptance — acceptance of their uniqueness of who they really are. The way they scream is as individual as they are. Some children withdraw, some act out, some overachieve, and some become delinquent. We need to look for the signs. It is my belief that this scream is universal. I would like to share a story with you that was written by a young man who was screaming out in his own unique way.

It was funny about school.
He sat in a square, brown desk
like all the other brown desks
and he thought it should be red.
And his room was a square, brown room.
Like all the other rooms.
And it was tight and close. And stiff.
He hated to hold the pencil and the chalk,
with his arm stiff and his feet flat on the floor,
with the teacher watching and watching.
And then he had to write numbers.
And they weren't anything.
They were worse than the letters that could be something if you put them together. . .
And the numbers were tight and square
and he hated the whole thing.
The teacher came and spoke to him.
She told him to wear a tie
like all the other boys.
He said he didn't like them
and said it didn't matter.
After that they drew.
And he drew all yellow
and it was the way he felt about morning.
And it was beautiful.
The teacher came and looked at his picture.
"What's this?" she said.
*"Why don't you draw something like Ken's drawing?
Isn't that Beautiful?"*

It was all questions.
After that his mother bought him a tie and he
always drew airplanes and rocket ships
like everyone else.

*Excerpted from "About School," a poem that was handed
to a Grade 12 English teacher in Regina, Saskatchewan.
Although it is not known if the student actually wrote it
himself, it is known that he committed suicide two weeks
later.*

This story reminds me to pay attention to what my children say or don't say and to what they express through their being. What do their eyes say? Do they need me to make a heartfelt connection? For so long when I looked into T.J.'s eyes all I saw was a glaze, a shell of who he once was. Now, his eyes speak volumes to me. I am aware of the unique gifts that my children possess. I try to encourage T.J.'s natural gifts. I let him express who he is with no judgment from me. He has learned that he can trust me and tell me anything. If I feel that what he has told me is unsafe or jeopardizes himself or someone else, I am very strong in my counsel and guidance. I can be extremely tough. I have to be. T.J. tends to push the envelope as far as I am willing to allow. In that context though, I realize that his reality is very different than mine. I can't judge all his perceptions because his experience is so unique to him. In keeping with my responsibility as his mother I will continue to be his strongest guide and advocate.

Another facet of T.J.'s healing process has been my realization of the limits of the current public education system. There are limitations in the amount of freedom teachers have to interact with T.J. on an individual basis. More often than not, they have to deal with too many students in the classroom, many of them as nutrient poor as T.J. was. They also have to deal with the fear of what is appropriate and inappropriate while working with these students. Fortunately, T.J. had a sixth grade teacher who didn't let protocol dictate how he related to T.J. This teacher would grab T.J. and playfully wrestle with him. At times, the only way to reach T.J. was through physical contact, so for us this teacher was a godsend. This may not hold true for your child. Perhaps physical contact is not appropriate in your child's case. What I would suggest is that you get to know your child and determine what works and what doesn't. Then, communicate this knowledge to the people working with your child.

For years I think T.J. was crying out for someone to see who he was. He doesn't fit very well into the educational system as it is currently set up. The way he learns does not conform to standardized curriculum used in public schools. He is very visual and artistic. He thinks in the form of symbols. School is not set up to accommodate his learning style. Both the school and I have gone through a lot of trial and error trying to find what seems to work for T.J. I am fortunate that I had all the necessary testing and reports that qualified T.J. for special services. I have been able to make certain requests of the school system and they are legally obligated to try to accommodate them. It is a catch-22, though, since the labels necessary for getting T.J. special help have also contributed to his lack of self-esteem. It is very confusing for T.J., because now that his body has done some healing, everyone is letting him know just how "normal" he actually is. T.J. doesn't believe he is normal. T.J. has always thought of himself as a "bad" kid, a bad seed. The switch from five years of perceiving himself as having problems to perceiving himself as normal will be an ongoing process. I have learned to let go of many of my expectations with regards to letter grades. We all know how intelligent he is. My hope is that he will learn to function socially and be happy with who he is as an individual. By the way, he is passing and doing school work at grade level without modification. This is a first in five years.

In November of 1995, T.J. began to write what he calls his songs. They are written from the perspective of a child who has lived with extreme mental conditions. By the time he was checked into the institutional hospital in 1993, T.J. himself wanted to get some answers. He wanted so much to fit in and behave like other children, but all the techniques we had tried to help him do that had failed. T.J. actually felt like he was crazy because what he felt on the inside didn't happen on the outside. He was feeling out of control of his own body. The fact that he had been living with physical tremors that he couldn't control compounded his frustration. What seemed like a last resort to find some answers became just another trauma for T.J. That time was devastating to our whole family. With T.J.'s permission I would like to share a song that he wrote in December 1995 about this experience. The words are his, the perspective his own.

Referral
by T.J. Sonner, age 12

Skulls coming at me.
Sick unto death I await my sentence.
One month in prison.
Ten years old, I want to die.
My hand begins to shake.
Jump out the window but it's plastic.
Why they hate me I don't know?
Is medication my fate?
My final day I await.
"Hospital"
Tears run down my cheek.

I gaze at the city.
Is this my tomb?
More tests.
A little boy cries down the hall.
They tell him to shut up and be quiet.
A demon comes to me in the night.
My bud sees his dead grandpa.
Purple fills the room.
"Hospital"
When I get out I'm babysitted by a queer.
Everyone doubts me.
"Hospital"

As I read this, I cried. This was one of the times I had not followed my gut instinct. My son's perspective is a harsh reality that I try to understand. His writing is a process of healing the wounds. He reassures me that his songs are just that, songs. He is sharing with me thoughts that have come to his mind without fear of my judgment. This is a great gift he is giving me. I get a glimpse of his reality. How can I not expand my own awareness? Social norms do not carry as much weight with me as they used to. How could they?

I have begun to ask some tough questions of myself, society, and our deeply ingrained institutions. Why do we seem to be losing our kids to anger, aggression, frustration, and even suicide? Are they loved? Are they physically healthy? Are they able to express their individuality? I don't have any concrete answers. All I know is that for my children, I will do what it takes to reach them. There are times when T.J.'s individuality is hard work for me. I have to keep in close contact with the people who work with T.J. I am as honest as I can be with them, T.J., and myself. We work as much like a team as we possibly can. I have been blessed with wonderfully caring people who are willing to keep an open mind when I share my thoughts and concerns with them. The road isn't always smooth, and we still hit a few bumps along the way. It is a continuous process, but then isn't that what life is like as a parent?

Recently, T.J. seemed to be struggling with school again. Things had been going along great and for some reason unknown to me, he started getting frustrated in his afternoon classes. In fact, on one of the difficult days, we received a call from his school. T.J. was not coping well, his frustration level was high, and he was causing some problems in his science class. The teacher and T.J. seemed to have hit a wall. When T.J. is in that state of mind, it is very difficult to reach him with reason. The walls are up and his brain doesn't let go easily. So when they called me, he had been sent to the principal's office. Rather than getting angry at T.J. and making him stay in school, we opted to just bring him home. I've fought that battle with T.J. many times and I have come to understand that when he is in that space of difficulty, he needs some distance from the source of his frustration.

My husband picked up T.J. and brought him home. We fed him some Omega Sun as soon as he walked in the door. Then my husband did something that I thought was brilliant. He asked T.J. to go write what he was feeling about what just happened at school. T.J. then looked very calm and immediately went to his room to write. Within ten minutes he was back downstairs with another song. His frustration had vanished and we were able to sit down and discuss what had occurred at school.

I don't always agree with T.J. or his perceptions, and I tell him so. But, in keeping with my expanded awareness of who he is as an individual, I validate what he shares with me. Let me share with you his perception of what happened at school. You may or may not like what he writes, but it is my belief that many of the children who experience similar difficulties have at one time or another felt the same way inside. The key is in teaching them constructive ways to cope with the feelings that come up for them. For T.J., eating more algae and writing this song helped to dissipate the intensity of the emotions he was feeling.

Blowing Up!
by T.J. Sonner, age 12

I've gotta' bad habit. Don't know why?
Was I born to blow up?
If I wasn't so whacked I could be normal.
But no, I'll never be the same.
If I could find my true meaning in life,
I would blow up!
My gut flyin', people cryin'.
Where am I gonna splat next?
My teacher is yellin'.
My nose is smellin' the stench on the wall.
I'm gonna blow up!
What if I'm just burnt extra crispy?
Or maybe, I blew up?
What if I was meant to be?
What if I was meant to cause havoc?
What if I was meant to blow up?
The unpleasant aroma of spit stenches
As I wipe off the gristle of my teacher's beef.
Maybe I should blow up?
Flustered is my middle name.
I'll blow up!!

Of course, by the time we were done talking T.J. was no longer "flustered" and calmly told us about the altercation between his teacher and himself. We discussed both sides of the issue. T.J. just happens to be a child who is perceptive of people's intentions. He knows without a doubt when someone doesn't like him or when they just don't want to deal with him. We've had different people tell him that they like him or that they want to help. If T.J. felt they were just going through the motions, he let them know it. That hasn't made it easy for me in trying to create teams of support for T.J. I remember when T.J. told one of the psychologists that the only reason this psychologist was concerned about him was because he was making ninety dollars an hour each time we went for a visit. There may have been some truth in that. The point is, no matter how much algae he eats or how much love, support, and acceptance I give T.J., there are parts of who he is as an individual that will always challenge some people. He doesn't back down, and I am proud of his honesty, even if it takes others aback or causes him trouble sometimes.

After this incident at school, T.J., the resource room teacher, and I discussed what options were available to help him through this difficult time. We decided to keep it simple. The only change we made was adding six capsules of Omega Sun to his routine at noon. The next day when T.J. came home after school he said, "I had a great day!" This was confirmed with a call from one of his teachers who said he didn't squirm any more than the other students, took notes, and participated well in class. Over the next week T.J. continued to function well. This teacher said she couldn't believe the difference adding more algae had made in his ability to function. She was impressed! I was relieved! I continually work at being flexible with situations as they arise. T.J.'s body has an ebb and flow that I try to stay in tune with so that when he needs more algae I add more, and when he needs less, I back off.

I am continually amazed at how big a change I see in T.J. when he has enough algae in his body. Over the three year period that we have been eating algae, I have been able to experiment with using different amounts of algae depending on T.J's state of mind. At times, he can be in a completely negative frame of mind and then I will suggest that he eat some more algae. Within minutes, I see relaxation come over his face. For T.J. this is not a fluke or random event. Finding something completely natural that gives him peace of mind has been, and is, a blessing.

T.J. is an extreme case, I know that. Don't get the idea that just because your child may not have the same problems, the things I have shared can't be applied. My daughter Brandee is a healthy, "normal" child in all respects. I have learned to include her in all the same "awarenesses" that I experience with T.J. She is excelling in the development of who she is as an individual. The algae has helped create an environment of balance in her body and she is seeing her own successes. With Brandee's permission, I would like to share with you her own algae story written in her words.

"My name is Brandee and I am nine years old. Since I've been eating the algae, my grades have improved. I can read much better. I was tired in school and now I am perky. At home, me and T.J. are getting along much better. I do not get as mad at T.J. when he does stupid stuff and bugs me. I have a better attitude. It has helped my dry skin spots. My hair seems shinier. At first I could not swallow the pills so I would mix a capsule in peanut butter and eat it. But then I figured out how to take them. Living with T.J. has been an *adventure!* Love, Brandee"

We can all benefit from taking care of our physical, mental, and spiritual bodies. Let's begin by educating ourselves to the possibilities and potential of who we as individuals are. Let's listen to our children who are screaming for recognition and acceptance. Let's do our job as parents to provide an environment of love and nurturing. Let's feed our children food that gives them the best opportunity for balance and health. What would it look like if the answers we were seeking were as simple as connecting with them through unconditional love, acceptance, and a balanced nutritional food like algae?

Let me share with you one of T.J.'s latest songs. You will see that even a child who has experienced so much difficulty in life can also in turn begin to experience so much joy.

Life
by T.J. Sonner, age 12

Water rushes as the white snow falls.
So much *"life"* upon this place.
Feeling of joy throughout my body.
My mind kicks in gear.
A sweet sting on my fingertips.
"Life"
A tree blows snow on me telling me hello.
The mountains are tickled with a blue aura.
"Life"
Have I been here before? The ground is moist.
A single branch sticks from the bottom of a tree.
"Life"
Could this be a place for humanity?
Something tugs on my paper,
trying to tell me something.
Maybe *"Life"*
A single tree sticks out from all the others
Like the ugly duckling yet — it's beautiful.
The rock which gives humanity a break
Is covered in white
"Life"

This song was written while T.J. was out in nature sitting under a tree. Do you understand my enthusiasm about our lives now? T.J. has gained a sense of connection to life and a sense of control over his own being and his own body. If he is feeling agitated he takes some Liquid Omega that helps calm him. If he needs to leave the classroom because it is too intense, he tells the teacher he needs to go to the resource room. He knows I don't expect him to be perfect. The hardest job I have is trying to help him see that he is a beautiful being and deserves all of my love and support. I will never give up on my convictions as a mother. I will be open to the many facets of who my children are. I will use all the resources available to me that will help guide them safely into adulthood. My point is that there is no hopeless child or hopeless situation. What seem like insurmountable odds can be beaten. One of the challenges we face is reaching our children before they feel all hope is lost. So, let's start now! There are many young lives that need to be touched with *hope*. Let me share with you some stories from other parents like me who have sought out answers for their children and found success. These successes are as varied as their children are. Somewhere in these stories, I know you will find a heartfelt connection.

Steven

Steven's struggle in life started early in my pregnancy. The doctor was not sure if he would go full term, or if he did, that everything would be okay. Thankfully, Steven's will for life took him full term, and when he was born he appeared to be a healthy little boy.

Once home, Steven was a very colicky and fussy baby. At first he only slept twenty to forty-five minutes at a time, day or night. Several weeks passed and he was still only sleeping two to three hours at a time. He didn't eat well and was not growing as fast as his older brother had. It seemed that he was always sick and fighting ear infections. We visited the doctor about every other week and the doctor would change antibiotics often so Steven would not become immune to one.

At around one year, the doctor diagnosed Steven with a well-known lung problem. His lungs were continually full of fluid. I was wondering if Steven would ever be healthy. His lung problems got so severe that when you held him, you could feel the rattle in his lungs through his back. You could hear him breathe from across the room. Steven was a real cuddle bug and always wanted to be held. He played very little and had no enthusiasm for life.

At this point, the doctor said that I would have to purchase a breathing-treatment machine. I was to give Steven three to four treatments a day. This was hard for me to think of doing, but I knew it was the only way to keep his lungs open.

The daily ritual of giving Steven his medication was also frustrating because he was forced to take so much of it. When I would get out the medicine dropper, he would run from me crying, "No, no!" I hated forcing the medicine into him. I had to hold him down and put his head between my legs. I would hold his arms under my legs so I could keep him from turning his head away or spitting the medicine out. I would wait to drop the medicine in his mouth between his gasping cries so that I would not choke him. On top of this horrendous experience, I was told that I would also have to trap him to give him breathing treatments involving *more* medicine (I chose to use a high chair.)

I didn't see or hear that the treatments were helping his problem to go away. They just made the symptoms easier for Steven to deal with. He would be fine as long as the treatments continued. I was completely frustrated. Steven still didn't sleep well and even if he slept, I didn't. I continually listened through the monitor to make sure he didn't struggle for air during the night.

There were times when I felt guilty about giving him all of that medicine. Would he have good feelings about me when I treated him this way? I tried to explain the situation to him, but what could a one and a half year old understand about this craziness? It was hard on those who helped me watch Steven because they had to go through the same process that I did. I could hear the hesitation in my mother's voice when I asked her to watch Steven. One of her first questions was always, "How many breathing treatments do I have to give him?" She did not sleep if he spent the night.

The worst experience I had with Steven was a night when he was feeling sick. As the evening progressed, so did his fever, rising to 103 degrees. He lay still on the couch with his clothes removed and I was trying to force liquids down him with a bottle. At 104 degrees and climbing, I was really worried and had been in contact with the local emergency room staff. They offered no advice but to continue watching him. If the fever got really high and the medicine did not break the fever, they suggested that I bring him in. I was waiting to see if the medicine would work and terrified the whole time as I watched his fever go up. At one point, I looked over at Steven — his still body and his glassy eyes. He managed to roll over and look at me. All he said was, "Bye bye, Mommy!"

We were in the car and on the way to the hospital in just a few minutes. Those twenty-five miles to the ER seemed endless as I talked to him, praying to God that he wouldn't die before I got help! Thank God, my prayers were answered, and after three hours in the ER, I took him home and held him all night long.

I was first introduced to Super Blue Green Algae by a friend. I tried the algae for myself, first. Then we decided to give the algae to Steven. Why not? I was totally frustrated with things the way they were and I hated all the medication I was putting into his little system.

Within the first week there were obvious changes. His body seemed to perk up and respond and he started to sleep better. In the next few weeks, I noticed that I couldn't hear him breath, his nose was running less, and he was not clinging to me all the time. He became very active and he got this little sparkle in his eyes that has never left. He started to play with his older brother and even began to play by himself.

For the first time since he was born, I have a real little boy and he is happy. My mother said, "He has a new lease on life!" With this new lease, Steven seems to be blessed with the ability to make others happy too.

One of the greatest things about the algae is that Steven eats it without a problem. He just puts the capsule or tablet in his mouth and chews it up until it's gone. If you forget to give him his algae he will ask for it. He knows there are different kinds and will ask for them by name. If someone gets algae out he will ask for it as if they had a bag full of candy. It only makes sense that he always knows what is best for him.

One time, my mother took Steven to the bedroom to put him to sleep. I heard her call for me so I went back to see what was wrong. She said, "Tell your mom, Steven."

He looked at me and said, "I can't go to sleep without my algae! I need my algae!" It's great hearing him ask for it.

I will never be able to explain how thankful I am or how much it means to me to have a normal, healthy boy. His body is back in balance and his lungs are clear for the first time in his life. A special thanks to very special friends who cared enough to share this wonderful food with us.

Sincerely,

Toni B.

Rexburg, ID

Mike

Mike is a seventeen year old who is a very helpful and usually cheerful son. At times, he has suffered from depression, mood swings, and behavior problems. We noticed early in his life that the slightest "stressful" situations at home and in school affected him greatly. Yet physical exams by our family doctors and finally a neurologist showed nothing amiss.

At the age of twelve, Mike began the popular method for treating his problem, medication. His ability to behave at school had grown increasingly difficult through the fifth and sixth grade. Without a supportive teacher in the sixth grade, he seemed to just fall apart emotionally. The methods we employed helped him function through the first two years of junior high.

Then, in the fall of ninth grade, he came to me and said, "I'm not feeling that much in control anymore, Mom." So, at the age of fourteen, Mike connected with a very helpful therapist and he began another course of action. His emotional and behavioral dysfunctions abated somewhat under supportive behavior modification counseling. However, Mike's sleeping problems continued. In August 1995, Mike (then seventeen and a junior in high school), made the decision to quit all therapies. We watched as his ability to focus and study and to maintain his "cool" at school and at home slid steadily downhill. He was extremely agitated with just about everything. He was beginning to discuss dropping out of high school and getting his General Education Diploma (GED) instead.

At the end of September 1995, he, along with four other family members living at home, began the Super Blue Green

Sure Start Program. Having everyone in the family eating the same little green capsules was a great morale booster for Mike. There wasn't something wrong with just *him!* The Sure Start program was a gentle way to begin. Since one doesn't take too many capsules at first, the slow, gradual increase worked well for Mike, an adolescent with growing concern about the effects of so called "pills" on his system.

Mike's agitation abated immediately. In the days and weeks that followed he had ups and downs depending on how consistently he ate his Super Blue Green Algae.

In our juggling to keep five algae consumers supplied, we ran out of enzymes. For a few days we ate the algae alone. Mike's depression and agitation increased dramatically! The day the enzymes were returned to his diet, he returned to a more balanced disposition and has responded well ever since. We have observed how difficult it is for Mike to remain consistent in his algae intake. When he's feeling good, he will often skip eating algae for a meal or even a whole day. We notice the effects the following day! I try to allow him to be in control. The whole point is to give Mike and my other family members tools and strategies that will serve them all the rest of their lives. (I do subtly herd him in the right direction when I see his mood dipping, however!)

One more thing I would like to mention is that Mike's dad and little sister also suffer with many of the same problems that Mike has. If I want to seriously make plans with Mike or his dad or his eleven year old sister concerning their depression, moodiness, or agitation, I choose times when they are fully tanked up with the nutritional benefits of Super Blue Green Algae products. They seem to listen and respond better. They process and assimilate the conversation and my input in a whole different, more productive way.

Sincerely,
Nancy H.
Troy, ID

One Year Later

Mike began his experience with Super Blue Green Algae in late September 1995. At that time, he had quit taking his medications for his focus, mood, and behavior problems. He was not functioning in the school setting and was talking about dropping out of school and getting his GED.

With the algae, enzymes, and probiotics, we saw an immediate improvement in Mike's mood and behavior. He not only stayed in school, but forged ahead. When a team of teachers, counselors, and the vice principal met with us at the beginning of second semester to review Mike's work, they all commented on his improved behavior and ability to stay in class. There had been no "incidents" requiring Mike to leave the classroom. One of the office staff voluntarily offered the comment, "How's Mike doing? I haven't heard him in the halls lately." In addition, his overall health improved. He did not experience his normal downtime with congested lungs or throat infections during the year.

Having passed all of his first semester classes, Mike added an early morning English class to his second semester. This was a makeup class from his dismal spring semester the previous year. He also signed up for the soccer team. In addition, he attended Boy Scout Troop meetings and took a class in kick boxing at the local health club two nights a week. We cautioned him about overdoing, and watched him struggle with an overload about two-thirds of the way through the semester. Still, he hung in there and passed all of his classes with better than flying colors. We give credit to very supportive teachers and leaders, but Mike was the one who got out of bed every morning and faced the music.

Mike worked during the summer of 1996 and was also involved with Scouting. He took his dad on thirty-five and fifty-mile backpacking trips in July and August. The two of them literally tore up the trails with their energy and leadership. Mike is in the first semester of his senior year. He plays varsity football and has completed an Eagle Scout Project. His project was to build a new floating dock for the swimming area in the Spring Valley Reservoir. The dock was made with cedar logs salvaged from flood runoff and redwood decking supplied by the local Lions Club. Last spring, he was elected to the office of the Lodge Chief of the Order of the Arrow, a Boy Scouts service organization, making him the senior youth leader in the Inland Northwest Council. He continues to give service in that office.

There are times when Mike feels overwhelmed by life and the various deadlines that he faces. Sometimes he even shuts down for an evening or a weekend. But, he seldom fails to fill his pocket carrier with algae and enzymes before heading out the door each morning. The result? A focused, determined, and often upbeat son coming and going around our house these days.

Sincerely,
Nancy H.
Troy, ID

Jamie

From the day our son Jamie was born, he has been easy to raise in every way. He is kind and gentle, thoughtful and bright. We could always reason with him and we shared an excellent rapport. At the age of fourteen, when he entered high school, all of that changed. It was like we had a different child. Everyone told us that he was a teenager now and that he would just be difficult for the next few years. That didn't make sense to us. We started looking for causes.

One cause was probably that as a child approaching adult height, Jamie felt that out of fear and misunderstanding society had started treating him with disrespect. Jamie noticed the change in how teachers now expected trouble from children the minute they entered High School. They read them the riot act, out of defense, causing the students to feel wrong and bad about themselves. Store clerks started watching for Jamie and his friends to steal. These were the same stores they had frequented with ease as smaller children. Even adults our age who shared the same ski mountain and skate park with us intimidated and manhandled Jamie and his friends in order to claim their space from these active teenagers. These causes of Jamie's drop in self-esteem were a little out of our control. All we could do as parents was to make Jamie aware of the fact that some adults have insecurities, and those insecurities sometimes show up in how they treat children and teenagers.

Another obvious difference was that he had grown six inches in the past year. When he came home from school, he went directly into the kitchen and ate everything in sight, including the condiments! This was one area where we knew we had some control. Understanding that our food is not what it used to be (I was born on a family farm), we were open to finding some viable whole foods that he could add to his diet.

The universe delivered! Our neighbor introduced us to Super Blue Green Algae. He had been eating Super Blue Green Algae for about three years and was at the peak of health in his late forties. Instinctively knowing the value of this whole food, Jamie, my husband, and I decided to eat it. I simply budgeted it into the grocery bill.

At this point, Jamie was miserable, lethargic, non-communicative, and very lazy. His grades at school had dropped off the bottom of the scale and he didn't even care.

Jamie started eating Omega Sun, the brain food. He ate one capsule a day. He couldn't swallow capsules at the time, so we opened them up and sprinkled the powder into his juice in the morning. On the evening of the third day (he had only eaten three capsules over a three day period), Jamie got up from the dinner table and stated that he "felt like rebuilding the front steps." Not wanting to discourage the sudden burst of energy and imagination, while at the same time not wishing to break a leg on a project that may take awhile and wasn't really necessary, we steered Jamie to building a much talked about footbridge over a stream bed in the backyard. Jamie began right away with wood left over from a previous project. He worked diligently for two days and built the most cleverly designed bridge. He filed the rough wooden edges and stained it light gray. *Amazing!*

A few days later we found him seriously cleaning out the garage. He was muttering to himself, "I can't believe I feel like doing this!" After that, he helped his Dad move a rock garden!

Since that day Jamie has been his usual sweet self. He has not stopped eating the algae. His grades at school are exactly where he chooses them to be. He is confident, ambitious, imaginative, and healthy. His allergy symptoms have disappeared. He does not get rattled by small stuff, and he is so pleasant to be around.

Jamie is nearing eighteen now and is a senior in high school. We let him eat whatever amount of algae his body wants. He can swallow capsules whole now. He sometimes eats up to seventeen Omega Sun capsules a day, a few Alpha Sun, Acidophilus when he feels a little under the weather, and Super Sprouts and Algae after he has had a full day of hard work or a day of snowboarding on the mountain. He totally values his body. There are two things that will carry him through life — his health and his word. Thanks to Super Blue Green Algae, we seem to have both covered.

It is not normal for teenagers to suddenly get a rough edge. There are a lot of factors that cause the change. Some we can control and others we can only be aware of. His diet is one area where we are in control, and adding SBGA to it has made a huge difference in our lives. Family life with this teenager is now pure joy every day!

Truly,
Jeannie C.
Ketchum, ID

One Year Later

It has been about three and a half years since Jamie began eating SBGA and other Cell Tech products. This time frame has been through most of his high school years. Throughout those school years, Jamie honored his body by not smoking, not experimenting with drugs of any kind, and never drinking alcohol. This is a pretty rare trait for a teenager moving into adulthood.

Since graduating from high school last June, Jamie has been pursuing what he enjoys the most. He has artistic talent that is presently expressing itself in the area of customizing cars. He spends most of his time at the shop learning his trade, and he is presently looking for a good shop to apprentice with.

Jamie continues to amaze us with his wisdom and calm outlook on life. He is a source of inspiration to us as he glides through life with what seems to be effortless knowledge that "where ever he is" is exactly perfect. He laughingly tells us that he calls this equilibrium the "Jamie Factor." We credit SBGA in part for his success in life. It keeps him balanced and centered. Everything else flows out of that!

Truly,

Jeannie C.
Ketchum, ID

Susan

Susan is a seven year old beautiful little girl. She has seen more trauma in her young life than any adult should ever have to. She was severely abused by her father at twenty to twenty-four months of age. He was verbally abusive as well as physically abusive. He threatened to kill both Susan and her mother. Susan suffered greatly because of this abuse. She was a normal child in her developmental stages up to this point. She was potty trained and she was talking in five to seven word sentences. When the abuse occurred, Susan's brain shut down her speech, she regressed in toilet training, and she began having seizures as often as twelve times a day.

Susan was removed from her father's presence. Over the course of the next five years she saw specialists of all kinds. Along with that came many theories about the origin of her problems. Some specialists admitted that they just didn't know. All of the testing that was performed showed no physical or biological reason for the seizure episodes. Nevertheless, the specialists tried to control Susan's seizuring through various methods. But the seizures never stopped, no matter what they tried.

Susan began to have severe side effects as a result of the seizuring and the methods they were using to control the fits. One of the most alarming trends was her loss of appetite. She just refused to eat. Susan lost fifteen pounds over a six month period, and our fear was that she would become anorexic. She also suffered from severe emotional problems. From January to June of 1995 she couldn't ride the bus to school because her behavior was so bad. She disturbed the other kids and driver. Her grandfather and I had to take her to school every morning. After school, she was permitted to ride the bus if she had the harness over her shoulders and the seatbelt buckled in and secure. Even then, at times, she caused trouble for the bus driver.

Finally, we decided to stop her treatment. We were extremely concerned about her weight. We had also noticed that somewhere along the line, Susan had forgotten how to smile and laugh because of the extreme hardships she had endured. We felt that she was malnourished, and our hope was that if we quit our current attempts to control her seizuring and behavior, she would regain both her weight and her joyful self.

One month later, we found out about Super Blue Green Algae. We decided to try it with Susan because we knew that she needed basic nutrition. Within five days we saw such a difference in her that we knew we were on the right track. The only change we had made in her life was adding algae to her diet. We started her on two Omega Sun and one Alpha Sun in the morning and then one Omega Sun in the evening.

Susan continued to improve all summer. Her thinking became clearer and we were able to reason with her. But best of all, she became a happy child and began to smile again. By summer's end, she had made the decision, all by herself, that she didn't want to wear the harness over her shoulders when she rode the bus. It was her choice and she was in control. She could behave and make good choices.

We are glad to say that the first semester of school is over and she has gotten along beautifully on the school bus this year. She continues to improve and is doing first grade work on most levels, especially math and spelling. Her reading is also coming along well. The teachers are amazed at the progress she has made. She has reached a state of physical and emotional balence and the seizure episodes are a rare occasion.

We thank God for answered prayers, for algae, for teachers who have cared so much, and for all who have taken an interest in Susan. Thank you Cell Tech, thank you Becki for introducing us to the algae. Thank you all! Susan is well nourished and has the potential to be a "normal" child again.

Sincerely,
Susan's grandmother
Darby, MT

One Year Later

I would like to add a personal note to this update on Susan. When I first met Susan, she was living with her grandparents. In the last year, it has been my pleasure to meet and become a dear friend to Susan's mother. Trauma had separated this mother and daughter for a while. What a blessing it has been to see them come back together again full of hope for the future. Susan's mother gives you this update, with much excitement, I might add!

Then, following are a couple of letters from two people who have worked with Susan. The first is from Susan's Kindergarten through eighth grade (K-8) School Counselor and the second is from her Special Education teacher.

Love,
Becki Linderman

Susan's mother writes:
Dear Becki,

I've been permanently reunited with my daughter Susan. It is so great to be back together!

In January of 1995 I had two options for Susan, send her to an institution or send her to her grandparents in Montana. Thanks be to God that I chose to send her to Montana. I'm grateful to her grandparents for being able to care for Susan for nearly a year. Thank you, Becki, for introducing us to Super Blue Green Algae.

In January of 1995 I was so scared for my daughter when I brought her to Montana. After being on medication for only six months for her behavior problems, Susan was as pale as a ghost. She looked like a walking skeleton with black rings around her sunken eyes. It was such a shock to see this little girl in a condition that caused her to act like a zombie. The medication had an incredibly detrimental effect on her physical strength and learning abilities. She had become too weak to ride her bike, pump a swing, or even hold a pencil to write. She had no ability to concentrate or reason, so academics were nearly impossible. Her mental alertness and capabilities were also hindered.

This past summer we have really seen a difference. Previously, Susan was unable to even smile while riding the new carousel in Missoula. Miraculously, after eating Super Blue Green Algae for only a few weeks, she began to smile and laugh, and was able to race for her favorite horse on the carousel, the black one with a beautiful rose, and manage to get to it before anyone else. She had a blast, being able to do so many more things. We went horse back riding, she rode a ten speed bike, and I taught her how to swim. She has quickly regained her strength and is now able to do what any other eight year old can do.

On the Fourth of July weekend we went boating on Lake Como with some friends. Susan had as much fun as she usually does when she goes to the lake, but this time something was different: I had Susan's full obedience. She obeyed me without screaming or fussing. She was also able to ride in an innertube all by herself.

It is such a pleasure to see the sparkle back in my child's eyes. I can't express it enough, the joy in my heart at having my missing child back.

At one time, Susan's body and brain were so out of balance from all the medication that she could barely function, but our doctors told us that that was the best we could do for her. All that seemed to be happening, though, was that instead of helping her, the treatment almost succeeded in destroying her.

Now, after three days of extensive testing in the hospital here in Montana, doctors have confirmed that Susan's seizures have ceased. On rare occasions, Susan still has seizure-like symptoms, but I believe that they are psychologically induced. Something will trigger a memory of past abuse or insecurity and she will have a seizure-like reaction.

Susan has been completely off all medication for a year and a half. She has been eating Super Blue Green Algae, the most nutrient dense food on the planet, all during this time. It is evident that her brain is being well fed. We are able to reason with her and I can carry on a normal conversation with her. Her concentration and comprehension are both so much better. She is able to memorize spelling words and even scripture verses. She is doing very well in school, bringing home "A's" and "B's."

All the children at school are also amazed with Susan because she is a different little girl. They are able to play with her now. Last year she would hit kids and scream constantly. Susan has come down a long hard road in life, but now that she is healthy, she will only keep on achieving more and more. I'm just so proud of her.

Susan was in a play earlier this year, *The Fisherman's Wife*, and of course she was the wife. She had such an excellent performance I couldn't believe my eyes. After seeing that and other things that she has achieved since eating the algae, I now know my daughter is going to do just fine in life. I truly thank Daryl Kollman for finding this awesome superfood! It has made such a remarkable change in Susan's life and my own. We will continue to eat Super Blue Green Algae for the rest of our lives.

I feel that I now have an obligation to reach out and help those parents who have similar problems with their children. I need to let them know that there may be an alternative that most parents don't know about, and it's *natural*. It's called Super Blue Green Algae!

Sincerely,
Susan's mother
Darby, MT

Susan's school counselor writes:

A school counselor has a unique opportunity to be personally involved in both the school and home lives of a large number of students. I have literally worked with thousands of interventions to help make students' academic, social, and personal lives better. One option I suggest to parents of tough kids who think they have tried everything is the use of algae. Algae is an option I have recommended to parents the last three years because I have personally witnessed the wonderful effect it has had on a number of our students.

One algae story seems to particularly stand out in my mind. Just after Christmas break in 1994, I registered a new Kindergarten student in our school. This child, Susan, had not been able to make progress in a specialized school for children with emotional and learning disorders in Illinois. Susan exhibited severe hyperactivity and tremors. Abuse had been prevalent in her past. She was at least two years behind grade level from the other kindergartners, and she was a year older. Susan had to be removed from the classroom on a regular basis because of her severe temper tantrums. She was so loud during these situations that she could be heard screaming from four or five classrooms away. These screaming sessions would often last half an hour. Susan's social skills were so seriously lacking that she was friendless and ostracized by her peers. At that time Susan was receiving dosages of two popular medications.

Susan's guardians were frustrated with the state their child was in. They decided on a different approach and started supplementing her diet with algae, hoping for the same success that other children in the school district had experienced with the algae diet.

Susan is now in the middle of second grade and our staff cannot believe she is the same person. She is now "mainstreamed" a little more than half of the day with her regular education peers. Behavior problems are becoming infrequent. She has not had a screaming fit in our school in more that a year. Her learning delay is rapidly closing the gap with her peers, and she now does much of the same work expected of any second grader. Her social skills were so lacking when she came to school than it is almost impossible to believe that Susan now takes an active roll in conflict resolution when she has a peer disagreement.

I am wise enough to know that it is not the algae alone that brought about these positive changes in Susan. A stable home life, abuse-free environment, good role models, and an outstanding teaching staff deserve a great deal of credit. Algae nevertheless had an impact in Susan's positive changes. This could be readily observed when the amount of algae Susan consumed was altered last year, resulting in Susan's experiencing the worst few weeks we had seen in months.

Susan is a success story that our staff is very proud of, and we look forward to Susan becoming a productive member of our society.

Sincerely,

Kurt Kohn, K-8 School Counselor

Susan's Special Education teacher writes:

In early 1994, five year old Susan was enrolled in our school—a rural school of approximately six hundred students, grades K-12. Although Susan was of Kindergarten age, she had not been enrolled in Kindergarten in her previous school primarily because of her very disruptive behaviors. Instead, she had attended a special-needs preschool.

We enrolled Susan in our special-needs preschool for half of the day and in our self-contained special education class for the other half. Susan's behavior was very disruptive and required additional adult help, even in a preschool setting. She often cursed, yelled, hit, bullied, ran away from staff, and exhibited a very short attention span and difficulty concentrating. Susan also experienced seizures. She was taking two medications to control hyperactivity and seizures. Even with the medicine and an individualized program, Susan's progress was limited. Then, in May 1994, Susan and her mother moved out of the district and Susan was enrolled in school elsewhere.

At her new school, Susan reportedly began exhibiting so many disruptive behaviors that the school was considering placing her in another special school. Susan's grandparents —prepared to do anything to help—offered to care for Susan and reenrolled her in our school. So Susan returned to us in January, 1995.

Although technically Susan was by this time enrolled in Kindergarten, because of her behaviors, very little Kindergarten curriculum was taught to her. We reenrolled her in Kindergarten in our school — but often she could not attend because of frequent hitting, yelling, jumping, and her inability to sit. Even though her medication seemed to help, "spiking" seemed to cause inconsistent results. We had to place Susan in the resource room for half of the day and in preschool for the other half. We hoped we could eventually move her into Kindergarten once again.

Although I have taught Special Education for over twenty years, Susan was a tremendous challenge. Susan was not able to control her behavior, attention, or concentration. She seemed to desire "negative" attention more than "positive" attention. If an adult entered my room to talk with me, Susan would scream loudly. She would scream so loudly and for so long that she would disturb all the classrooms in the hall. There was no place to take her in our school where she couldn't bother others. Fortunately, my room was by an outside door and the weather was warming. I would take her outside until she quieted. Removing her from presence of others was the only effective consequence I could use with Susan.

We provided summer tutoring for Susan. This was helpful, but because of her limited attention and concentration, progress was very slow. Even by July, Susan could not consistently identify letters, sounds, and numbers. Academically, she was perhaps at mid-Kindergarten level. Socially, she seemed lower. Her mother had tried, her grandparents were trying very hard, and the school was trying—even hiring a one-on-one aide to be with her during part of the day.

Her grandparents were worried. Even with extreme intervention, Susan still had limited success learning. She ate very little and her health seemed poor. One week when I went to tutor her, Susan was unable to work at all and was extremely fidgety, wiggly, and defiant. Grandma said they had taken her off her medications because of all the side effects. I understood their concerns, but yet I wondered, "How will Susan learn without the pills?"

Then I learned that her grandparents had begun giving Susan SBGA and were hoping it would help her. The next week, I was skeptical when I tutored Susan, but I noticed definite improvement. So I thought, "This is worth a try."

As time passed, the school staff and I noticed even more improvements. Summer ended and Susan started school again, attending first grade for half a day and spending the rest of the day in the resource room. She became a happy and eagerly accepted member of her class. She wanted "positive" attention, so she tried to sit quietly. She attended class, was polite, and could actually interact with other children.

I noticed that as Susan continued to eat her algae, her concentration steadily improved, as did her learning ability. Many staff and students could not believe that she was the same little girl. She even looked different! Her eyes seemed to lose that "wild" look, she began to eat again, gain some weight, and appeared healthier. During first grade, Susan remained in class and completed first grade Math, Science, Social Studies, Music, Physical Education, and Library, as well as Language Arts instruction in the resource room. We were delighted that at the end of first grade Susan tested at mid first grade level in Reading. Yes, she was behind her peers — but look how far she had come! Plus, her behavior was so improved that an aide to monitor her behavior was rarely needed.

Now, Susan is in second grade. She still strives for "positive" attention, works hard, and can often monitor her own behavior. She still continues to learn.

I am a teacher and I believe that our school has worked hard and provided Susan with an excellent education. I also believe that her grandparents and mom deserve much praise for their love and dedication. At one time, we were all uncertain and confused about Susan's behavior and learning — until Susan started eating algae. The algae is the foundation of our effort to help Susan build academic, social, and appropriate behavior skills. Without that foundation, progress is slow, limited, and inconsistent. The algae allows Susan to

work to her potential. That's what learning and life is!
    Sincerely,
    Susan VanGoye, Special Education Teacher

Scott

Scott's learning disabilities became noticeable in first grade. He had a hard time focusing when there were any distractions. Yet he could not be described as hyperactive because he was very calm and mild mannered. We thought the solution to his distraction would be to send him to a private school with small class sizes. We did this, yet he still had difficulty concentrating. In second grade his teacher requested that we have him tested. He was diagnosed as a visual learner. He did not process auditory instruction in the same way as the average, mainstream student. He was also characterized as very artistic, with a lot of gifts on the visual side. We enrolled him in therapeutic sessions geared at helping him to compensate. This was important because most instruction methods used in traditional education lean heavily towards verbal/auditory techniques.

Scott still struggled. In third grade he transferred to a Waldorf School. The Waldorf method is full of art-based, hands-on, interactive projects which seemed to fit his learning style. He did well in Waldorf. However, test taking remained difficult for him and his teacher described him as exceptionally dreamy.

He graduated from the Waldorf School in the eighth grade. In ninth grade he began his journey in the public school system. He set forth on this journey in a very positive way. He was ready for a change. That summer he took a speed reading course. I was determined to give him every opportunity to be successful. Since he was active in sports, he already had several friends in his new school. He is a very organized and self-disciplined young man, so everything should have gone well after the initial adjustment period. But it didn't! Socially, he was happy. He was playing soccer and had a few close friends. That suited him fine. Academics, however, were traumatic. Despite constant and great effort on his part, his grades were coming up "C's," "D's," and "F's." He began to feel demoralized. We engaged tutors for the two classes he was having the most difficulty with. The results were minimal. The day he came home and said, "I guess I'm just stupid," I knew that something had to be done right away. This was becoming a self-esteem issue. We looked into home-schooling. However, Scott was really enjoying the adventure of high school and wanted the experience. The next step seemed to be conventional treatment. I was so desperate that I began to research the use of medicine to help my son focus.

It was at this juncture that Scott became ill with a very deep chest cold. He missed four days of school. The doctor put him on antibiotics. He recovered enough to return to school. (He hated missing even a day.) The deep cough persisted and he was exhausted all the time. He endured another round of antibiotics to no avail.

It was at this time, on the brink of deciding to put my son on medication to regulate his ability to concentrate, in the midst of a health crisis, that Super Blue Green Algae was reintroduced into my life. I had signed up the previous summer, eaten the algae for about a month and thought, "No big deal." My sponsor called me up and encouraged me to give it one more try. She is a very dear friend and I trust her. So, I reordered. I also read the book *August Celebration* (available from Cell Tech) for the first time. I had been a Montessori teacher for nearly ten years, so I could really relate to Daryl's story. Light bulbs went flashing in my brain. I was so excited that I cried. (Previously, I had been crying from heartbreak for my son.)

As soon as the algae arrived, Scott began eating it. He willingly participated in our experiment. The first noticeable effect was that his cough began to diminish. He began to feel more energetic and was less moody. I'll never forget the day, after three weeks of eating algae, he came home waving three papers. He called out "Mom! Look what's happened since I've started the algae." He produced three pages of work, all marked with an "A." They were from his computer class. Previously, he had had great difficulty in that class. It required a lot of concentration. A student must be able to listen to the teacher and punch in commands on the computer. He was at a low "D" level in that class. He found it so discouraging because at home he was quite adept with the computer. This was in April. As time went by his grades steadily improved. One day in his science class (where he had been maintaining a failing grade), his teacher patted him on the back and asked him what had changed, because his grades were improving dramatically.

The end result of his freshman year in high school was that his grades rose to "B's" and "C's," and he got an "A" in P.E. His morale was high and my prayers had been answered. Recently, he received his grades for the first semester of his sophomore year. To our delight, he has a "B" average and is on the honor roll. I am filled with gratitude for the gift of the algae and that my sixteen year old son is a dedicated algae eater.

Sincerely,
Ann T.
Novato, CA

Postscript: I have three other children, ages four, six, and eleven who also eat algae daily. I have observed improved health and calmness in them all.

Tim

Tim is a thirteen year old who is learning challenged and has some behavior problems. When he came to stay with my husband and me in the summer of 1995, he was unhappy about the course of action his step-father had taken in helping him to deal with his problems. He said it was not doing him any good because he was falling asleep all the time. He was falling asleep in class, out of class, and at home. We decided that while he was staying with us we would give him a break and see how he did. About that time, I met Becki and she introduced me to Super Blue Green Algae. We decided to let Tim try it. He was only with us for a short time, but in that time we saw big changes in him. He really liked the algae.

My husband and I were able to sit down with him over the summer and help him with his homework without a big fight. He seemed to comprehend things fairly well. He told us that school was fun now, that he enjoyed his classes and schoolmates, especially T.J. Tim is a very good kid and likes to make friends. The other kids seem to like him too.

The resource room teacher worked with Tim several hours each day at school. She knew him before he began eating algae, and she got to see his progression while he ate it. She told us that she felt that the algae was making a difference in his ability to focus and pay attention. His school performance was improving as he got healthier with the proper nutrition.

Tim is a hardworking child at home. He loves people easily and loves life itself. Tim sets high goals for himself and he just needs love and guidance to help him get where he wants to go. I know how hard it is to get there, because I have learning disabilities myself. The difference can be in how hard you work for what you want and how much support you have. Tim and I worked hard to make some of his goals a reality. I looked for options to help him succeed. The algae was one of those options.

Kids like Tim and T.J. need nutrition, love, understanding, time, patience, and togetherness to be able to pull their lives together and function. With God's help and hard work, those goals can be met. Incidentally, I am eating the algae too and I'm now working on getting my GED.

Today, Tim is back with his stepfather and he chooses not to give Tim algae. When I talk to Tim, he says he would really like to eat algae again. I hope that day is coming soon.

I am Tim's mother. I love him and I want the best for him. I am also a friend to T.J. I will do anything I can to help these kids work through their rough pasts. I have seen the positive changes that can happen, and I look forward to seeing good come to both of them. I hope to see them both get diplomas and graduate, grow up and have happy lives of their own. I know that they will give back to us the love and support we have given them. Thank you for this opportunity to share my hope.

God Bless!
Terri D.
Darby, MT

R.J.

In the spring of 1995, I read a small article in a magazine about memory and attention potentially being affected in a positive way by products from Cell Tech. There was no phone number, but I took down the information and proceeded to find out more about the products. My greatest motivation was my fourteen year old son, R.J., who has learning and behavior problems. After years of tests, doctors, and medications that were not effective, I was looking for something that would help him. I also wanted something to help the whole family. For anyone who has not lived with a child who has these problems, count your blessings. It is about the most chaotic, disorderly way of living you can imagine. In my opinion, my husband also has these kinds of problems, yet he managed to survive the system because in the past people followed a slower life-style with less stress. My son, however, has not been so lucky. School has been very difficult. Little was known about these problems ten years ago when he entered the school system. Even though there is a little more knowledge now, most teachers and school administrators just advise more discipline.

As I heard stories from other people and learned more about the algae, I became anxious to give it a try. I placed our first order, and R.J., his two younger brothers, and I started taking acidophilus capsules. Then we began introducing both the Alpha and Omega algae into our diets. At first I was watching so hard that I did not notice what was happening. Sometimes it is the absence of a problem that helps you to see.

For instance, R.J. has always had tremendous eye-contact avoidance. Along with his learning and behavioral problems, he also has many other physical and mental challenges that manifest as repetitive rocking, chewing, and other movements. Soon after adding algae to his diet, however, we began having conversations eye to eye. He began to sit on chairs without rocking, told me things just once (instead of several times), and sat quietly during dinner.

At the same time, I noticed a change in the rest of our home life. All three of my children (who have more than the normal amount of sibling rivalry) began interacting and working together. For the first time I felt a sense of calmness and togetherness in our home.

R.J. was actually helping his youngest brother with school projects, getting his chores done without a lot of argument, and staying on task with his school work. He seemed to have greater control of himself and a positive awareness of how his actions affected others around him. I felt a sense of calm and peace in our home that had never before been present. This sense continued for days and days. It was wonderful!

The positive changes in my son were so obvious that people who did not know him very well were commenting on the differences they were seeing. Even the testing administrator at our neuropsychologist's office commented on the change in R.J.'s behavior when he went for his annual office visit.

Unfortunately, R.J.'s father cannot or will not give the same recognition to what was happening. Sadly, as a result of my husband's negative attitude and comments, my son will no longer eat the algae. We are back to the same disruptive behaviors and family chaos. The rigid set of R.J's jaw, his angry looks, eye avoidance, difficulty staying on task, and so many more unhealthy problems have returned. And the answer is so *simple*.

When we began our experience with algae, I read numerous articles on the subject of nutrition, especially how nutrition affects the human body and the importance of amino acids. What I learned was amazing, and I am determined to educate my son, who is well aware of his differences and many of his difficulties, about the need to provide himself with proper nutrition. The algae made it so simple. *Hope springs eternal.* I can only hope that I will soon be able to say that my son is again eating algae. I look forward to regaining the peace and calm that we once had in our home.

On a positive note, I continue to eat the algae. I find I am able to handle our home situation and the ever present stress much better than in the past. I have far more energy and better control of my own emotions. It is my hope that this account will inspire others to explore nutritional alternatives, as I found in the algae, for both themselves and their children. Sharing information seems to be the best first step, and so I am happy to share what I have learned. As anyone with a child like mine knows, it is very easy to lose yourself as you fight their battle for them. It is a difficult task, but if we don't take action and try, who will?

Sincerely,
Rebecca T.
Blackfoot, ID

Todd and Emily

Dear Becki,

I would like to let others know how our lives have changed due to meeting you, Becki, and finding out about Super Blue Green Algae.

We first heard about SBGA at a support group meeting for parents. You shared your story of how algae helped your son T.J. when all other efforts had failed and the system had given up on him. You shared this with us because some of the parents had asked if you knew of any alternatives to conventional treatments. I was open to your suggestions because I believe that there are times when natural methods can be found and tried before resorting to conventional medication. I am not condemning those who find help with the conventional system, but I wanted to see if there might be another way to go before diving into that method of treatment.

My husband and I adopted two children, Todd and Emily, ages three and four. Each has a genetic background of alcohol and drug abuse. We knew that their futures could be difficult, not only for them but for us as well. They were both very hyperactive children, to say the least. Some of their behavior problems manifested as violent tempers, minimal attention spans, self-mutilation, sleep problems, and other negative behaviors.

We had been working on behavior modification methods and did see some improvements. Our feeling was that we would never be really successful in using this method alone. Whenever we thought things were improving, our family would take a major slide downhill again. We were getting desperate and feeling like failures. We love our children very much, so when we heard of SBGA, we wanted to give it a try.

We started slowly, giving each child one capsule of Omega and one capsule of Alpha in the morning. Within the week we were seeing a difference in their attention spans. After the first week, we added one Omega at noon to their diets. We noticed that they fought less and wanted to cooperate for the first time. After two weeks, we added an additional Omega in the morning and started noticing that Emily, the oldest, was grasping ideas that she was never able to before. Todd became much less violent and wanted to be hugged more. Both of them started going to sleep at a normal hour.

At the present time, they each eat two tablets of Omega in the morning and afternoon and one tablet of Alpha in the morning. The changes in them are noticeable to everyone who knows us. Many people have made positive comments on their behaviors and have asked us what we are doing.

There was a time when I wondered if the algae was really doing anything. Isn't it amazing how easily we forget just how "bad" it was? It's especially easy to forget when life seems to be going along okay. One day, I ran out of algae and couldn't get any for several days. By the time I was able to get more algae, I had *no doubt* that it made a difference. I thought I was going to go nuts with all the negative behaviors that returned within a forty-eight hour period. By the end of three days, it was horrible trying to stay sane in our house. What a blessing to see the algae arrive.

You would think that after that experience I would never doubt the algae's benefit again, but I guess I'm a slow learner! At one point, I hoped that since the children had finally experienced good behavior, they would continue to improve on their own. Wrong again! I now realize that the algae is an integral part of helping them continue to grow and enjoy life.

I'm not trying to say that algae is a miracle cure, but if we hadn't found out about it, I can't imagine where our family would be right now. The struggle had gotten so bad that our marriage and family were being tested to their limits.

Once someone asked us if it was good to have our children eat something that they may have to eat for the rest of their lives in order for their bodies to be in balance. I thought about this and finally decided that I *do* hope that my children will want to monitor their diets and eat healthily in hope of keeping their bodies balanced and healthy for the rest of their lives. There is nothing wrong with commiting to good nutrition. And while they may decide someday not to continue eating algae, for now, the algae is helping them and there is no way that that is bad!

I started using SBGA myself and find I have fewer problems with my attitude and I am less tired. Another family member, who has an extremely stressful medical job, is eating it and seems to be able to go longer hours and retain more of his studies at the same time.

Thanks to SBGA we just finished taking our first real vacation to visit family members. It was a success. I would never have thought of flying in a plane for hours and touring various attractions, day after day, without the algae. The one thing we made sure we packed was plenty of algae!

We now have hope for our new children. Before the algae, we had wondered if Todd and Emily would be able to have friends because of their behavior problems. We are not expecting angels. At least they can now comprehend our teachings and they have a chance at learning and growing in a healthy way.

Sincerely,
D.B.
Hamilton, MT

One Year Later

Well, it's been about a year since I last told you about our two little ones, Todd and Emily, and I thought you might appreciate an update on their progress. It's hard to really know where to begin. We have seen so many wonderful improvements over the past year. They still have temper tantrums, and yet our children are able to control themselves with only a look or a reminder from me. Their learning ability has jumped in leaps and bounds.

For instance, we own a computer and Todd, now four, and Emily, five, both use many of the learning programs we bought for them. The other day Todd was at the computer and I wondered what he was doing, since I hadn't put anything in for him. Then I realized that he must have remembered how I had started his learning game before. He managed to put the CD in, find the appropriate program, and get the game up and running all from memory! I think I could be in for trouble in a whole new and wonderful way!

A few weeks ago, Emily was talking to Daddy and asked, "Daddy, why do some people always minimize things?"

Well, Dad wasn't sure if she knew what the heck she was saying, so he asked her to explain. She said, "You know, Daddy, like if someone gets good grades — like all "A's" and a person says, 'Oh big deal!'"

I don't know about you, but I don't know too many five year olds who think like that! We never have a day go by without something like that happening. I truly believe that SBGA has allowed their minds to open up and function as God intended.

I teach a class for children at church, so I see lots of children each week. What really made me see what algae has done for my little ones is a special little boy in my class. I have infants through first graders in my room. This little boy is four years old and definitely a candidate for algae.

Each week I watch this precious little boy try so hard to sit still and listen. We do plenty of activities to work out the wiggles, so it's not like I expect him to sit for an hour. He can sit for about thirty seconds and then he just *has* to jump up and tell me a story or grab me and tell me he loves me or do *something* other than sit still. Of course, he constantly tries to engage Todd in some activity, and yet now I see my child trying to ignore it and listen carefully. Two years ago I would never have dreamed that my children would be the ones behaving and being the helpers in class!

I am going to try to share our experience with the little boy's parents. I know the youngster doesn't want to act naughty, but he truly can't help himself. To watch him is like going back in time, seeing my own children struggling not to be naughty, and yet always seeming to be doing the wrong thing at the wrong time.

Todd's and Emily's behaviors continue to improve, and yet there are still times when I forgot to give them algae and we all pay the price. One day we had gone to town and unexpectedly stayed for lunch with a friend. I didn't have any algae with me because I planned to go home for lunch. At around one, the kids starting "acting out" and even my friend noticed the drastic change in their behaviors and attitudes. I looked at her and said, "It must be around one or one-thirty isn't it?"

She said, "How do you know that?" I explained that if we go an hour past their regular time for the algae I can see the difference. Sure enough, it was one-thirty! My friend is now a believer in what SBGA can do for my children, and I keep bottles of algae in the glove box of every car!

We have begun doing some schoolwork here at home. Emily asked me to write out the alphabet and her name for her. She kept the piece of paper and the next day walked out and said, "Look Mommy, I spelled my name!" Sure enough she had spelled her name correctly and very neatly too. She then proceeded to write down the letters of the alphabet and tell me what they were! This is the same child who over a year ago couldn't remember the simplest of instructions less than five minutes after receiving them.

Now, during Sunday school my little ones are the only children who can answer all my questions and tell multiple Bible stories. The other parents are extremely impressed. If only they knew all the facts, they would be even more impressed. I hope that I haven't given the impression that I expect our children to turn into perfect little models. It's just that I now see them able to function in the world at their fullest and not be ridiculed for behaviors that they can't control. Sure, there are days when they are cranky and irritable, but who doesn't have those? At least now we can enjoy growing and learning together rather than struggling to just get through the day.

Recently I took Todd and Emily on a weekend trip by myself. We drove for hours and sang songs and had a pleasant journey. At the resort they were so good I kept wondering if it would last. One evening I thought I'd take them into the formal dining room and we'd have a "special" dinner. It would be a night for learning special manners and getting all dressed up. I was so proud of them I could have burst! They got to put juice in their wine glasses and use good china. Boy, did they have fun. I had more people complementing me on my beautiful, well-mannered children than I ever dreamed possible.

I give you this story not only to show how proud we are of our children's continuing improvements, but also to show how SBGA has helped to enhance our children's world. I truly believe that without the algae, they would not be able to experience half of what they have because of all the unstable behaviors they used to exhibit. And while there is so much more to say, I'll end this letter. I just thought you might like a brief update to help encourage others to hang in there!

Sincerely,

D.B.

Hamilton, MT

Closing

My goal in writing this book and sharing these testimonials with you is to let you know that there are always options and that you never need to give up hope. Options are presented to us all the time. We can see them if we are just paying attention. This book is an option. Algae is an option.

Perhaps you will gain some insight from what is shared herein. Maybe you have read something you can try that will support you and your child as you walk through the challenges presented in your life. What I share of my own and other parents' experiences with you comes from my heart. If there is even one child and family who is helped because of my story or the stories of others, then all of our families' trials have not been in vain. Our children are screaming. Are we ready to listen?

Recently, T.J. was asked to write a song of hope. His perception of hope is very different than mine. He wrote it and then I asked him to explain a few things to me. The way he writes is very symbolic and some of his symbols are personal to him, so I will share with you what he told me.

What he talks about first is being in an institution. The word destruction means medication, institutions, negativity, and emotional pain. He then gets out of the institution, but still has no answers. The friend he talks about is Dolora, my sponsor in Cell Tech as well as T.J.'s first real connection to another person outside of his family. What he needed was unconditional love, acceptance, and algae. The word "it" refers to his hyperness, anger, fear, etcetera. The rest of the song I know you will understand.

Host To Destruction?
by T.J. Sonner, age 12

I am NOT a host!
Host to destruction.
The air smells like gasoline.
I shall scream into the abyss of lights.
Look out the window.
Locked away inside.
Where they gonna put me next?
Am I damned or am I hexed?
Shall I pray for what I need?
If I get what I need I won't be a host.
A host to destruction!
Now I'm tweaked and besieged.
No one knows what I need.
Then a friend reaches out,
Takes my hand.
Now, It's out! The curse is gone!
No more pain or sorrow.
Now I live for tomorrow.
I'm okay now for life.
My soul is still cut with their knife.
But, I believe I'm not a host anymore.
NOT a Host to destruction!

My family and I wish you and your loved ones success in your journey toward health and well-being. Whatever avenue you decide to take, know that there are other parents and care-givers out there trying to share their hope with you. Many networks and teams are in place just waiting for you to make the connection. You already have the courage, you live or work with a complicated child!

Resources That Have Been Valuable to Me

Audio Tapes

Title: "How to Get Your Child and Teen to Pay Attention in School and Behave at Home" by Pete Buntman, MSW, ACSW. (Also available as an updated 1996 version.)

Synopsis: Pete Buntman, from The Center for Family Life, Inc., interviews parents, children, doctors, and educators on how the algae impacts their lives. The Center will donate ten cents from the sale of each tape to the Cell Tech Solution.

Price: Available in multiples of 25 starting at $1.25 each. Accepts VISA, Mastercharge, Discover, and American Express.

To Order: Call "The Fulfillment Center," Video Plus at (800) 388-3884.

Title: "Big D's Little d's For a Lifetime of Health" by Dr. Ron Meyers

Price: $3.00 audio cassette, $3.50 soft cover booklet

Synopsis: This is a good resource for learning more about the algae itself — what it is and how it affects the body at a cellular level.

To Order: Contact Ransom Hill Press at (800) 423-0620.
Volume discounts available.
Not Cell Tech approved material.

Title: "Hope For Our Children." (An International Teleconference Call.)

Price: $.65 each

To Order: Available from Cell Tech, order code #2057.
Cell Tech approved material.

Title: "The Miracle" by Daryl Kollman.

Synopsis: "The Miracle" expresses the heart of the Cell Tech vision and relays the tremendous impact of SBGA.

Price: Up to 49 are $1.00 each

To Order: Available from Cell Tech, order code #2085.

Cell Tech approved material.

Books, Booklets, and Articles

Title: "Kids Eat Algae Too, Vol. II " by JoeJo Gittelman.

Synopsis: A guide to using algae with children. Contains important resource material. A percentage of the price of this booklet is contributed to the Cell Tech Solution.

Price: $15.00 each. Soft cover book. Send check or money order and include $3.00 shipping for the first book *plus $.50 for each additional book.*

To Order: Mail order and check/money order to:

Brian Associates, Inc.

P.O. Box 205

Glenbrook, Nevada 89413

Cell Tech approved material, approval #095079.

Title: *Fifty Algae Stories* by Lisa Moore, DC

Synopsis: *Fifty Algae Stories* is filled with true stories about children, adults, the elderly, and animals who have experienced spectacular benefits from eating SBGA.

Price: $12.95 each. Soft cover book.

To Order: Contact Ransom Hill Press at (800) 423-0620.

Volume discounts available.

Cell Tech approved material, approval #99750.

Title: Network of Hope Newsletter

Synopsis: This newsletter is dedicated to proactively helping families with school-age children.

Price: $25.00 US or $29.00 Canadian for a one year subscription.

To Order: Please write:

Network of Hope

PO Box 701534

St. Cloud, FL 34770-1534

Cell Tech approved material.

Title: *Guidelines to Feeding Super Blue Green™ Algae to Children, Revised Edition* by Pete H. Buntman, MSW, ACSW.

Synopsis: Author Pete H. Buntman is a Licensed Clinical Worker and Cell Tech Double Diamond. Ten percent of the proceeds will benefit Network of Hope Feeding programs.

Price: $3.00 each

To Order: Please write:

Center for Family Life
3611 Farguhar Ave., Suite 3
Los Alamitos, CA 90720
Fax: (310) 596-4601
Cell Tech approved material, approval #100069.

Title: *August Celebration* by Linda Grover

Synopsis: Full length book detailing the story of Daryl and Marta Kollman and how they came to create Cell Tech.

Price: $4.00 each

To Order: Available from Cell Tech, order code #8000.
Cell Tech approved material.

Title: *Help for Moms with Hyperactive Kids: How to Live With Your Teenager, Vol.I.* Subtitled, "A Survivor's Handbook For Parents" by Pete Buntman, MSW, ACSW

Title: *How to Live With Your Teenager, Vol.II.* Subtitled, "A Question and Answer Guide" by Pete Buntman, MSW, ACSW

To Order: For more information, write to:

TN Trading
10566 Garden Grove Blvd.
Garden Grove, CA 92643
Not Cell Tech approved material.

Title: "The Nicaragua Report" published by Cell Tech

Synopsis: This is a study of the effects of SBGA on the nutritional status and school performance of first, second, and third grade children attending the Monsenor Velez School in Nandaime, Nicaragua.

Price: $25.00 for ten booklets

To Order: Available from Cell Tech, order code #2018.
Cell Tech approved material.

Title: "The Children and Algae Report" by The Center for Family Wellness, Claudia Jewett Jarratt, Director

Synopsis: This report is the result of a nationwide research project investigating the effects that the consumption of algae by children has had on academic performance, social interaction, and problematic behaviors.

Price: $5.95 each. Add $1.75 shipping for one copy.

To Order: Color Print
610 Court Street
Clearwater, FL 34616
Telephone: (800) 962-6300
Cell Tech approved material.

Title: *ALGAE from Upper Klamath Lake: The Ultimate Superfood* by Andrew Paterson

To Order: For more information, please write:
Body Balance Center
21901 Erie Lane
Lake Forest, CA 92630
Not Cell Tech approved material.

Title: "Don't Dine Without Enzymes" by Victor P. Kulvinskas, M.S.

Price: $2.25 each

To Order: Available from Cell Tech, order code #2024.
Cell Tech approved material.

Title: *Mental Illness: Not All In The Mind,* edited by Patrick Holford
Synopsis: This is a Mental Health Project publication supported by The Institute for Optimum Nutrition.
To Order: Please write:
Blades Court
Deodar Road
London, England, SW15 2LR
Tel: 0-181-871-2949
Not Cell Tech approved material.

Title: *A.D.D. Attention Deficit and Hyperactivity: A Nutritional Action Plan* by Mel Boyd
Synopsis: Shows how improved nutritional status will change lives. This is a "how to" booklet. Includes checklist for eight basic nutritional changes.
To Order: Please write:
Mel Boyd
New Perspectives
Communications, LTD
2116 2nd Ave. So.
Minneapolis, MN 55404
Not Cell Tech approved material.

Title: "Hope is a Molecule" by Daryl Kollman.
Price: $1.75 each
To Order: Available from Cell Tech, order code #1046.
Cell Tech approved material.

About the Author

Becki Linderman was raised in Eastern Idaho. She is married and has two children, Brandee, eleven, and T.J., thirteen.

Although licensed to practice Landscape Architecture, Becki's life was pulled in a different direction when she discovered that her son T.J. suffered from  attention and hyperactivity problems. This discovery threw her into a whirlwind process of educating herself and her family about her son's special needs and the ways in which they could be met. In February 1993, Becki discovered Super Blue Green Algae from Cell Tech. Since then, she has become active with Cell Tech and with spreading the word about algae. She also maintains a network of friends who also have special needs children. Together, they share their stories and pass on words of hope and encouragement to one another. Becki's utmost desire is to plant the seeds of hope, and to help others see the beauty of who these "complicated" children really are.

Complicated Child?
Simple Options

Item #CC $10.00

**BUY IN BULK
AND SAVE $$$**

Complicated Child?
Simple Options

DEEP DISCOUNT BULK PRICING!

2-3 copies .... $8.50 each book
4-5 copies .... $8.00 each book
6-9 copies .... $7.50 each book

10 PACK BONUS

1 ten pack............$7.00 each book
2-5 ten packs.......$6.00 each book
6-10 ten packs.....$5.00 each book
11+ ten packs.....$4.50 each book

Name: _____ Check / Credit Card:

Address: _____

City: _____ State: _____ Zip: _____ Ph:( ) _____

Name on credit card: _____

Credit Card #: _____ Exp. Date: _____

Signature: _____

Qty.	Item#	Title	Price	Total
	CC	Complicated Child? Simple Options		

SHIPPING:*

If Subtotal Is:	Standard	Priority
$10.00 or less.............	$2.95	$5.00
$10.01 to $20.00.........	$3.95	$6.00
$20.01 to $50.00..........	$5.95	$8.00
$50.01 to $75.00..........	$6.95	$9.00
$75.01 to $100.00.......	$7.95	CALL
$100.01 to $150.00.......	$9.95	CALL
$150.01 to $200.00......	$11.95	CALL
$200.01 or more add 7%		CALL

Make checks payable to:
**Ransom Hill Press PO
Box 325 Ramona, CA
92065**

* Shipping to AK, HI, P.R., outside
of the USA, UPS, C.O.D. & RUSH
Orders, please call for price.

Subtotal:	
CA residents add 7.75% sales tax:	
Add shipping:	
Total Enclosed:	

Ransom Hill Press
1-800-423-0620
FAX: 1-619-789-1582

Outside of USA call (619) 789-0620
Prices subject to change without notice.

Featured Titles

Big D's Little d's For A Lifetime of Health

Dr. J. Ronald Meyers
Item #DMT $3.00 sample cassette
Item #DMB $3.50 booklet.

In this audio cassette or booklet, Dr. Meyers

gives you critical information on what your body needs to get and stay well. He and his patients have found that eating blue-green algae has decreased their daily symptoms and increased their chances for a lifetime of health.

Fifty Algae Stories

Lisa Moore, DC
Item #50AS $12.95

Read the miraculous testimonials of more than fifty adults, children, and animals who have experienced dramatic changes in their health as a result of eating this ancient superfood, Super Blue Green Algae. This is a great book for educating yourself about the many illnesses algae has helped. Many stories include photos.

Simple, Cheap and Easy: How To Build A Cell Tech Business Off Your Kitchen Table

Venus Andrecht
Item #SCE $9.95

Simple, Cheap and Easy teaches you everything you need to know to make your Cell Tech business thrive! It was written *just* for Cell Tech distributors, and leads you step-by-step through the process of approaching people with the algae and then quickly signing them as distributors.

Call for volume discounts.